Spanish

Aladdin Books
Macmillan Publishing Company
New York

© 1989 by **BERLITZ PUBLICATIONS, INC.**, a Macmillan Company
866 Third Avenue, New York NY 10022

Aladdin Books
Macmillan Publishing Company
866 Third Avenue, New York, NY 10022
Collier Macmillan Canada, Inc.

First Aladdin Books edition 1989

Printed in USA

3   5   7   9   10   8   6   4   2

Published as a worldwide co-edition in collaboration with
Dami Editore, Milano
Illustrations by Tony Wolf

Library of Congress Cataloging–in–Publication Data

Berlitz Jr. Spanish—1st Aladdin Books ed.
p. cm.— (Teddy Berlitz)
English and Spanish.

Summary: Teddy Berlitz introduces basic phrases, the alphabet,
numbers, and colors in Spanish accompanied by a cassette that
incorporates music, sound effects and the voices of native speakers.
ISBN 0-689-71315-0

1. Spanish language—Conversation and phrase books—English—
Juvenile literature. (1. Spanish language—Conversation and phrase books—English.)
I. Berlitz Schools of Languages of America. II. Series.
PC4121.B527 1989
468.3'421—dc19   88-37261
                                                                              CIP
                                                                              AC

To the parent:

Learning a foreign language is one of the best ways to expand a child's horizons. It immediately exposes him or her to a foreign culture—especially important in a time when the world is more of a "global village" than ever before.

Berlitz Jr. is the first Berlitz program of its kind. Like the adult language programs that Berlitz pioneered, the Berlitz Jr. teaching method is based on clear and simplified conversations, without the need for grammatical drills. Within minutes, just by listening to our sixty-minute cassette and following the beautifully illustrated text, your child will be saying a few simple but invaluable foreign phrases.

Your child will love Teddy and enjoy meeting his family and friends. Together you and your child can follow Teddy to school, where he learns how to count and spell, and then on to playtime in the park and a visit to the circus. All you have to do is listen and repeat. You will hear native speakers saying each phrase clearly. There is a long pause after each phrase so that your child can repeat it, imitating the authentic pronunciation. Music and sound effects add to the fun.

All the phrases on the cassette are found in the book, together with a translation, illustrated by lively and appealing drawings. And if you want to find the exact meaning of a word quickly, just look it up in the foreign-language vocabulary at the back of the book. The book and cassette reinforce each other but can be used separately once your child is comfortable with them.

All children have the potential to speak a foreign language. By using frequently repeated words in a storybook form, Teddy Berlitz allows children to tap that potential. These carefully constructed texts have been approved by school language-experts and meet the Berlitz standard of quality. Best of all, the book-cassette format enables a new language to be learned in much the same way your child first learned to speak.

Enjoy sharing Teddy Berlitz—and watching your child's world grow.

Berlitz Publishing

¡Aquí está Teddy!
Here's Teddy!

¡Hola! Me llamo Teddy.
Hello! My name is Teddy.

Soy un oso.
I am a bear.

Hablo español.
I speak Spanish.

Y tú, ¿hablas español?
And you? Do you speak Spanish?

Sí   No

Yes   *No*

No hablo español.
I don't speak Spanish.

¿Hablas inglés?
Do you speak English?

Sí  No

Yes *No*

Sí, hablo inglés.
Yes, I speak English.

Me llamo Teddy.
My name is Teddy.

Y tú, ¿cómo te llamas?
And you? What's your name?

¡Perdón! ¿Puedes repetir tu nombre, por favor?
Excuse me! What's your name again, please?

Me llamo...
My name is...

¡Gracias!
Thank you!

Esta es mi casa.
This is my house.

Mi casa está en el bosque.
My house is in the forest.

Mi casa es pequeña. No es grande.
My house is little. It isn't big.

Hay muchos árboles y muchas flores en el bosque.
There are many trees and many flowers in the forest.

El bosque es bonito.
The forest is beautiful.

Este es mi papá.
This is my daddy.

Esta es mi mamá.
This is my mommy.

Quiero a mi papá.
I love my daddy.

Quiero a mi mamá.
I love my mommy.

Quiero a mis padres.
I love my parents.

Mis padres dicen "hola" también.
My parents say hello, too.

Tengo una hermana.
I have a sister.

Tengo un hermano.
I have a brother.

Mi hermano se llama Pedro.
My brother's name is Pedro.

Mi hermana se llama María.
My sister's name is Maria.

Soy grande.
I am big.

Pedro y María son pequeños.
Pedro and Maria are little.

¡Ellos son niños pequeños!
They are babies!

Pedro, María y yo tenemos muchos juguetes.

Pedro, Maria, and I have many toys.

Tenemos:
We have:

un tren,
a train,

una pelota,
a ball,

una muñeca,
a doll,

un coche,
a car,

un avión,
a plane,

un barco,
a boat,

un cubo y una pala.
a pail, and a shovel.

Nos gusta mucho jugar con los juguetes.
We like to play with the toys very much.

Esta es mi escuela.
This is my school.

Mi escuela está en el pueblo.

My school is in the town.

Voy a la escuela los lunes, los martes, los miércoles, los jueves y los viernes.
I go to school on Monday, Tuesday, Wednesday, Thursday, and Friday.

6
SABADO

7
DOMINGO

No voy a la escuela los sábados
ni los domingos.
I don't go to school on Saturday and Sunday.

Hoy es lunes. Voy a la escuela.
Today is Monday. I am going to school.

Esta es mi clase.
This is my classroom.

Esta es mi maestra.
This is my teacher.

¡Hola! Soy la señorita Rosa.
Hello! I'm señorita Rosa.

Dile "hola" a mi maestra.
Say hello to my teacher.

¡Hola!
Hello!

Esta es Pepita.
This is Pepita.

¡Hola!
Hello!

¿Es Pepita una maestra?
Is Pepita a teacher?

No, Pepita no es una maestra.
No, Pepita is not a teacher.

Ella es una alumna.
She is a student.

Pepita está leyendo los números.
Pepita is reading the numbers.

Uno, dos, tres, cuatro, cinco, seis, siete, ocho, nueve, diez.

One, two, three, four, five, six, seven, eight, nine, ten.

Vamos a contar del uno al diez.
Let's count from one to ten.

1 2 3 4 5 6 7 8 9 10

¿Puedes contar con Pepita?
Can you count with Pepita?

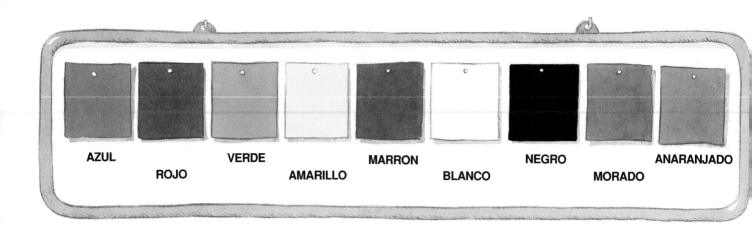

AZUL · ROJO · VERDE · AMARILLO · MARRON · BLANCO · NEGRO · MORADO · ANARANJADO

Este es Carlos. Estos son los colores.

This is Carlos. These are the colors.

Azul, rojo, verde, amarillo, marrón, blanco, negro, morado, anaranjado.

Blue, red, green, yellow, brown, white, black, purple, orange.

¡Yo sé escribir!
I know how to write!

Escribo A, B, C...
I'm writing A, B, C...

Mira, estoy escribiendo el alfabeto:
A, B, C, CH, D, E...
Look, I'm writing the alphabet: A, B, C, CH, D, E...

Ahora leo el alfabeto:
Now I'm reading the alphabet:

A, B, C, CH, D, E, F, G, H, I, J, K, L, LL, M,
N, Ñ, O, P, Q, R, S, T, U, V, W, X, Y, Z.

Deletreo mi nombre: T-E-D-D-Y.
I'm spelling my name: T-E-D-D-Y.

Teddy. ¡Soy yo!
Teddy. That's me!

¿Puedes deletrear tu nombre también?
Can you spell your name, too?

Cantamos en la escuela.
We sing at school.

Esta es una canción.
This is a song.

¿Quieres cantar con nosotros?
Would you like to sing with us?

¡Vamos, canta con nosotros!
Come on, sing with us!

Fray Felipe…
Fray Felipe…
Brother Philip…
Brother Philip…
¿Duermes tú?
¿Duermes tú?
Are you sleeping?
Are you sleeping?
Suena la campana…
Suena la campana…
The bell is ringing…
The bell is ringing…
Din, don, dan,
Din, don, dan.

¡Bien! ¡Muy bien!
Good! Very good!

Niños, ¿Qué hora es?
Children, what time is it?

¡Son las tres!
It's three o'clock!

¿Es la una? No.
Is it one o'clock? No.

¿Son las dos?
Is it two o'clock?

No. ¡Son las tres! ¡Bien!
No. It's three o'clock! Good!

Termina la escuela.
School is over.

¡Adiós, señorita Rosa!
Good-bye, señorita Rosa!

ESCUELA

¡Adiós, Teddy!
Good-bye, Teddy!

¡Adiós, Pepita!
Good-bye, Pepita!

¡Adiós, Carlos!
Good-bye, Carlos!

La sorpresa
The Surprise

¡Vamos al parque!
Let's go to the playground!

Nuestro parque favorito está cerca de la escuela.
Our favorite playground is near the school.

Se pueden hacer muchas cosas en el parque.
You can do a lot of things in the playground.

Vamos al tiovivo.
Let's go on the merry-go-round.

Estoy en el columpio.
I'm on the swing.

¡Mira, bajo por el tobogán!
Look, I'm going down the slide!

A las cuatro volvemos a casa.
At four o'clock we go home.

Camino hacia el bosque.
I walk to the forest.

Camino por la carretera.
I walk on the road.

Veo un cartel en un árbol.
I see a poster on a tree .
El cartel dice "Circo".
The poster says: "Circus".

Parece divertido.
It looks like fun.

Y cuando llego a casa – ¡sorpresa!
And when I get home – surprise!

Teddy, ¿te gustaría ir al circo?
Teddy, would you like to go to the circus?

¿Al circo? ¡Sí, claro! ¡Vamos!
To the circus? Oh, yes! Let's go!

El sábado, mamá me lleva al circo.
On Saturday, Mommy takes me to the circus.

Pedro y María se quedan en casa con papá.
Pedro and Maria stay home with Daddy.

El circo está cerca del parque.
The circus is near the playground.

La carpa del circo es azul y roja.
The circus tent is blue and red.

Todo el mundo hace fila.
Everybody is standing in line.

¡Hola! Me llamo Julia.
Hello! My name is Julia.

Me llamo Teddy.
My name is Teddy.

Este es mi hermano Jaime.
This is my brother Jaime.

Vamos a sentarnos juntos.
Let's sit together.

¿Hay cocodrilos en el circo?
Are there crocodiles in the circus?

No, pero hay leones.
No, but there are lions.

¿Hay jirafas en el circo?
Are there giraffes in the circus?

No, pero hay cebras.
No, but there are zebras.

Hay monos.
There are monkeys.

¿Cuántos monos?
How many monkeys?

No lo sé. Vamos a contar: uno, dos,
I don't know. Let's count: one, two,
tres, cuatro, cinco, seis. Seis monos.
three, four, five, six. Six monkeys.

Veo un elefante. ¡El elefante es grande!
I see an elephant. The elephant is big!

¡Mira, hay dos payasos!
Look, here are two clowns!

¡Uno está contento, el otro está triste!
One is happy, the other is sad!

¡El desfile! ¡Qué desfile más grande!
Here's the parade! What a big parade!

¡Mira cuántos animales!
Look at all the animals!

Después del circo compramos un helado.
After the circus we buy ice cream.

Quiero chocolate.
I want chocolate.

Quiero fresa.
I want strawberry.

¡Y yo quiero vainilla!
And I want vanilla!

Jaime, ¿dónde vives tú?
Jaime, where do you live?

Vivo cerca del parque.
I live near the playground.

¿Vas a la escuela aquí?
Do you go to school here?

Sí.
Yes.

Entonces podemos jugar a la salida de la escuela.
Then we can play after school.

¡Adiós, Jaime!
Good-bye, Jaime!

¡Adiós, Teddy!
Good-bye, Teddy!

Vocabulary

A

a—to, at
    a las cuatro—at four o'clock
    Voy a la escuela.—I go to school.
¡Adiós!– Good-bye!
ahora—now
al (a + el)—to the, on the
    Vamos al tiovivo.
    Let's go on the merry-go-round.
alfabeto—alphabet
alumna—student
    Ella es una alumna.
    She is a student.
amarillo—yellow
anaranjado—orange
animales—animals
aquí—here
árbol(es)—tree(s)
avión—plane
azul—blue

B

bajo—I go down.
    ¡Mira, bajo por el tobogán!
    Look, I'm going down the slide!
barco—boat
¡Bien!—Good!
billetes—tickets
blanco—white
bonito—beautiful
bosque—forest

C

camino—I walk
campana—bell
canción—song
¡Canta!—Sing!
cantamos—we sing
cantar—to sing
carpa—tent
carretera—road
cartel—poster
casa—house
cebras—zebras
cerca—near
    cerca del parque
    near the playground
cinco—five

circo—circus
claro—of course
    ¡Sí, claro!—Oh, yes!
clase—class, classroom
coche—car
cocodrilos—crocodiles
colores—colors
columpio—swing
    Estoy en el columpio.
    I'm on the swing.
cómo—what
    ¿Cómo te llamas?
    What's your name?
compramos—we buy
con—with
contar—to count
contento—happy
cosas—things
cuando—when
cuántos—how many
    ¡Mira cuántos animales!
    Look at all the animals!
cuatro—four
cubo—pail

CH

chocolate—chocolate

D

de—of
del (de + el)—of the, from
    cerca del parque—near the playground
    Vamos a contar del uno al diez.
    Let's count from one to ten.
deletrear—to spell
deletreo—I spell, I'm spelling
desfile—parade
después—after
dice—he/she/it says
    El cartel dice "Circo".
    The poster says: "Circus."
dicen—they say
diez—ten
dile (di + le)—say, tell him/her
    Dile "hola" a mi maestra.
    Say hello to my teacher.
divertido—amusing, fun
    Parece divertido.
    It looks like fun.

domingo(s)—Sunday(s)
dónde—where
dos—two
duermes—you sleep
    ¿Duermes tú?—Are you sleeping?

gustar—to like
    Nos gusta mucho jugar...
    We like to play very much...
    ¿Te gustaría ir al circo?
    Would you like to go to the circus?

E

el—the
elefante—elephant
ella—she
ellos—they
en—in
entonces—then
es—he/she/it is
    Esta es mi casa.
    This is my house.
escribiendo—writing
    estoy escribiendo—I'm writing
escribir—to write
escribo—I write
escuela—school
español—Spanish
ésta—see **éste**
está—he/she/it is
    Mi escuela está en el pueblo.
    My school is in the town.
éste, ésta—this
    Este es mi papá.
    This is my daddy.
    Esta es mi mamá.
    This is my mommy.
éstos—these
    Estos son los colores.
    These are the colors.
estoy—I am

F

favor—favor, kindness
    por favor—please
favorito—favorite
fila—line
    Todo el mundo hace fila.
    Everybody is standing in line.
flores—flowers
fray—friar, brother
fresa—strawberry

G

gracias—thank you
grande—big

H

hablar—to speak
    ¿Hablas español?
    Do you speak Spanish?
    No hablo español.
    I don't speak Spanish.
hace—he/she/it does
    Todo el mundo hace fila.
    Everybody is standing in line.
hacia—to, towards
hay—there are
    Hay monos.—There are monkeys.
helado—ice cream
    helado de chocolate—chocolate
    ice cream
hermana—sister
hermano—brother
¡Hola!—Hello!
    Dile "hola" a mi maestra.
    Say hello to my teacher.
hora—hour, time
    ¿Qué hora es?—What time is it?
hoy—today

I

inglés—English
ir—to go

J

jirafas—giraffes
jueves--Thursday
jugar—to play
juguetes—toys
juntos—together
    Vamos a sentarnos juntos.
    Let's sit together.

L

la, las—the
leo—I read
    Ahora leo el alfabeto.
    Now I'm reading the alphabet.

leones—lions
leyendo—reading
    Pepita está leyendo los números.
    Pepita is reading the numbers.
lo—it
los—the
lunes—Monday

LL

llamarse—to be called
    Mi hermana se llama María.
    My sister's name is Maria.
    ¿Cómo te llamas?
    What's your name?
    Me llamo Teddy.
    My name is Teddy.
llego—I arrive
    Y cuando llego a casa...
    And when I get home...
lleva—he/she takes
    Mamá me lleva al circo.
    Mommy takes me to the circus.

M

maestra—teacher
mamá—mommy
marrón—brown
martes—Tuesday
más—more, so
    ¡Qué desfile más grande!
    What a big parade!
me—me, myself
    Me llamo Teddy.
    My name is Teddy.
mi, mis—my
    Quiero a mi papá.
    I love my daddy.
    Quiero a mis padres.
    I love my parents.
miércoles—Wednesday
¡Mira!—Look!
    ¡Mira cuántos animales!
    Look at all the animals!
mis—see **mi**
monos—monkeys
morado—purple
muchas—see **muchos**
mucho—a lot
muchos, muchas—many
    muchos árboles—many trees
    muchas flores—many flowers

mundo—world
    todo el mundo—everybody
muñeca—doll
muy—very

N

negro—black
ni—neither, nor
niños—children
no—no
    No lo sé.—I don't know.
nombre—name
nos—us
    nos gusta—we like
nosotros—we, us
nuestro—our
nueve—nine
números—numbers

O

ocho—eight
oso—bear
otro—other

P

padres—parents
pala—shovel
papá—daddy
parece—it seems, looks like
    Parece divertido.
    It looks like fun.
parque—park, playground
payasos—clowns
pelota—ball
pequeña, pequeños—little
    Mi casa es pequeña.
    My house is little.
    Pedro y María son pequeños.
    Pedro and Maria are little.
¡Perdón!—Excuse me!
pero—but
podemos—we can
por—for, on
    por la carretera—on the road
    por favor—please
pueblo—town
pueden—you/they can
puedes—you can
    ¿Puedes deletrear tu nombre?
    Can you spell your name?

Q

qué—what
quedan—they stay
    Pedro y María se quedan en casa.
    Pedro and Maria stay at home.
quieres—you want, like
    ¿Quieres cantar con nosotros?
    Would you like to sing with us?
quiero—I want, love
    Quiero chocolate.
    I want chocolate.
    Quiero a mi mamá.
    I love my mommy.

R

repetir—to repeat
    ¿Puedes repetir tu nombre?
    What's your name again?
roja, rojo—red

S

sábado(s)—Saturday(s)
salida—exit, way out
    a la salida de la escuela
    after school
se—oneself
sé—I know
    ¡Yo sé escribir!
    I know how to write!
seis—six
señorita—Miss
sentarse—to sit down
    Vamos a sentarnos juntos.
    Let's sit together.
sí—yes
siete—seven
son—they are
    Ellos son niños pequeños.
    They are babies.
    ¿Son las dos?
    Is it two o'clock?
sorpresa—surprise
soy—I am
    Soy un oso.
    I am a bear.
    ¡Soy yo!
    That's me!
suena—it rings
    Suena la campana...
    The bell is ringing...

T

también—also, too
te—you, yourself
    ¿Cómo te llamas?
    What's your name?
tenemos—we have
tengo—I have
termina—it ends
    Termina la escuela.
    School is over.
tiovivo—merry-go-round
tobogán—slide
todo—all, every
    todo el mundo—everybody
tren—train
tres—three
triste—sad
tu—your
tú—you

U

un, una—a
uno—one

V

vainilla—vanilla
vamos—we go
¡Vamos!—Come on! Let's go!
    ¡Vamos al parque!
    Let's go to the playground!
vas—you go
    ¿Vas a la escuela aquí?
    Do you go to school here?
veo—I see
verde—green
viernes—Friday
vives—you live
    ¿Dónde vives tú?
    Where do you live?
vivo—I live
volvemos—we go back, return
    A las cuatro volvemos a casa.
    At four o'clock we go home.
voy—I go

Y

y—and
yo—I